ALTERNATOR
BOOKS™

MISSION
HTML

SHEELA
PREUITT

Lerner Publications ◆ Minneapolis

TO MY MOTHER, VASANTHA SUBRAMANIAM,
FOR HER IMMENSE LOVE AND GENEROSITY

Lerner Publications Company
A division of Lerner Publishing Group, Inc.
241 First Avenue North
Minneapolis, MN 55401 USA

For reading levels and more information, look up this title at www.lernerbooks.com.

Main body text set in Aptifer Slab LT Pro.
Typeface provided by Linotype.

Library of Congress Cataloging-in-Publication Data

Names: Preuitt, Sheela, author.
Title: Mission HTML / Sheela Preuitt.
Description: Minneapolis, MN : Lerner Publications Company, [2020] |
   Series: Mission: Code (Alternator Books) | Includes bibliographical
   references and index. | Audience: Age 8–12. | Audience: Grades 4 to 6.
Identifiers: LCCN 2018044354 (print) | LCCN 2018045135 (ebook) |
   ISBN 9781541556393 (eb pdf) | ISBN 9781541555914 (lb : alk. paper)
Subjects: LCSH: HTML (Document markup language)—Juvenile
   literature.
Classification: LCC QA76.76.H94 (ebook) | LCC QA76.76.H94 P75 2020
   (print) | DDC 006.7/4—dc23

LC record available at https://lccn.loc.gov/2018044354

Manufactured in the United States of America
1-46047-43463-4/4/2019

CONTENTS

To download files for the Your Mission: Code It! activities, visit http://qrs.lernerbooks.com/HTML. Save the files in My Documents. You will also need text-editing software. Windows computers usually come with Notepad, and Mac computers usually come with TextEdit. Always check with an adult before downloading files from the internet.

CRACK THE WEBSITE CODE

What kinds of websites do you usually visit? Maybe you use a library website to look for your favorite book. Or perhaps you look up restaurant menus before you eat at new places. If so, you have been using a powerful code-breaking tool on your computer that lets you view these websites!

The next time you look at a website, try this: Right-click anywhere on the page, and then select View Page Source. You'll see a bunch of unfamiliar text. This text is written in a code called hypertext markup language (HTML). You may not be able to read this gobbledygook, but your web **browser** can use those instructions to display the content in a way you can understand.

How does your computer browser know what to show on a restaurant website? A coder uses HTML to tell it!

CHAPTER 1

WHAT IS HTML?

HTML IS A KIND OF CODE. Coders write web page content in HTML so that any web browser can understand and display the content. HTML code is made up of step-by-step instructions that a browser follows.

A web browser is a program that locates, accesses, and displays websites. Popular web browsers include Internet Explorer, Firefox, Chrome, Opera, and Safari. Each has its unique features, but they all use HTML to display web pages.

🔒 https://www.nasa.gov/kidsclub/index.html

PROTOCOL DOMAIN PATH HTML FILE NAME

A website is a collection of web pages that belong together and are stored on the same computer.

The World Wide Web is a vast but scattered collection of **resources**, such as text files, digital photos, audio files, and videos, stored in different computers in different parts of the world. HTML adds structure and formatting to these resources. That makes the resources show up on-screen in a way that people can easily read.

Are you ready to write some HTML?

Anyone can write HTML once they figure out the basics. It's not just for professionals.

CHAPTER 2
GETTING STARTED

TO CREATE HTML, YOU WILL NEED A COMPUTER WITH A WEB BROWSER AND A TYPE OF PROGRAM CALLED A PLAIN TEXT EDITOR. The text editor that comes with Windows machines is Notepad. Mac computers come with the text editor TextEdit.

First, open the *HTML Files* folder you downloaded from the **URL** listed on page 3.

Open your text-editing program. From the File menu, open *blank.html* in the *HTML Files* folder. Then type the following text into the blank file:

```
<!DOCTYPE html>
<html>
<head>
<title> Hello and Welcome,
Everyone</title>
</head>
<body>
Hello and welcome, everyone!
This is my first web page.
</body>
</html>
```

From the File menu, select Save As. Save the file with the file name *welcome.html* in *HTML Files*.
Go to the *HTML Files* folder and double-click on *welcome.html* to open it in your default browser.

The information in angle brackets in HTML does not show up when you open a page in your browser. But it does tell your browser how to display the information.

Congratulations! You have created an HTML file. Let's understand the HTML. The words enclosed in < > are called tags. The five tags you used in *welcome.html* must be included in every web page.

<!DOCTYPE html> is always the first line in every HTML document. This tag tells the browser what type of document you're making.

Every element of HTML needs an opening tag. The opening tag at the beginning of this file, <html>, marks the start of the HTML code. A closing tag, </html>, marks the end of the HTML. The opening and closing tags look the same, except for the forward slash / used for the closing tag.

Next, your web page needs a title. To tell the browser that the title shouldn't show up on the web page itself, put the title tags inside the tags <head> and </head>. The title should clearly describe the page's content, because it will show up in search results, as well as in the browser tab and toolbar when someone bookmarks your page. But the title won't display on your actual web page. Use the opening and closing tags <title> and </title>.

You'll put your main content in the <body> so visitors can see it. End the section with </body>. Your audience will be able to see what is inside the body tags.

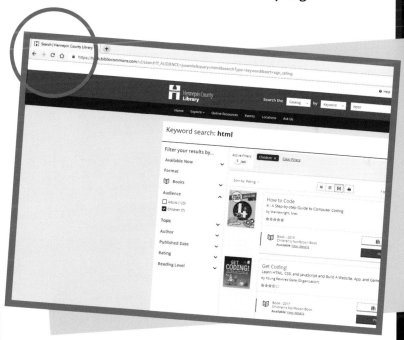

The title of your web page displays on the browser tab in the upper left corner of the screen.

Other tags tell your browser how to display different types of information. Headings, which start new sections, catch the eye and group content into pieces. **Search engines** use headings to index the content of your web page.

When you type keywords into a search engine, it checks the headings of many web pages to find content that matches your terms.

Your website can include several headings. Location, size, and style are some of the ways a site shows the importance of headings.

You can use six different heading tags. <h1> and </h1> represent the biggest, most important heading. A heading tagged with <h2> will be a little smaller and less important, and so on until <h6>.

Use a paragraph tag <p> to mark ordinary text. The <div> tag shows a division, or section, of the page and can be used as a box, or a container, that holds different kinds of content.

The unordered list tag <ul> displays the text as a bulleted list. In the HTML, each list item is enclosed in list tags: <li>. An ordered list tag <ol> is used for a numbered list, with each list item enclosed in <li>.

All of these tags will give your web page text. But you may want to make some text look different. You can use formatting tags for that. One example is <strong>. That makes the text bold. It also tells a search engine that this element of the page is important.

```
<!DOCTYPE html>
<html>
<head>
<title> Example of bold text
formatting</title>
</head>
<body>
<strong>This text is bold
</strong>
</body>
</html>
```

The HTML formatting tag <strong> makes text bold on a web page.

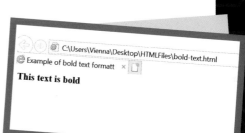

CODE IT!

In your text editor, open the *books.html* file you downloaded from the URL on page 3. Use what you learned about creating HTML files in Chapter 2 to edit and save the HTML.

Change the title of the web page to "My Favorite Books."

Change the <h1> to a different heading tag, and replace the heading text with "Welcome to my books page!"

Edit the book list to show your five favorite books using the ordered list tag.

Save the file as *mybooks.html* in the *HTML Files* folder.

Then double-click to open the *mybooks.html* file in your browser. Do you see your five books ordered from 1 to 5? If not, review your code. Can you find what went wrong?

CHAPTER 3

ADDING LINKS AND IMAGES

HOW DO LINKS AND PICTURES FROM OTHER PLACES ONLINE END UP IN THE SAME WEB PAGE? HTML tells your browser where to find the files, as well as which files to use. Use the <img> tag for images. An anchor tag <a> will add a link to another site.

Each tag in the previous chapter had an opening and a closing tag. But some tags, including <img>, do not need closing tags. They're called singletons.

If the image file and the .html text file are stored in the same place (such as your computer), then your HTML will include the image file name, called the relative URL:

```
<img src = "california-sea-lions
.jpg">
```

An **attribute** provides more information that tells the browser how to display the content within the tag. The src attribute in the above example points to the

Putting the relative URL or the absolute URL in your HTML will tell your browser where to find an image you'd like to display.

location or path for the image file. Other attributes give different kinds of information, such as how wide or tall the image should be on the web page.

If you want your page to link to an image stored on another website, you'll use the site's full, or absolute, URL for the image source:

```
<img src = "https://upload.
wikimedia.org/wikipedia/
commons/3/3e/Sea_lion_%28close
-up%29%2C_Vancouver_
Aquarium_%283179841840%29.jpg" >
```

Be sure to ask permission before using anyone else's photos on your web page. Using them without permission is stealing.

Browsers ignore blank spaces and line breaks in the .html file. But you can insert spacing by using HTML tags and special character codes. The <br> tag adds a line break. So

 adds two blank lines. You can add extra blank space within text with the HTML character code * *.

The most powerful feature that connects the "web" of the World Wide Web is the way HTML documents can be linked to one another by a clickable URL. You do this by using the anchor tags <a> and </a>.

The attribute href points to the target destination, using either the full absolute URL or the relative URL if the target is on the same website.

Sometimes you want to use special symbols on your web page. These HTML character codes will tell your browser to display these symbols.

Let's add website links to your *animals.html* file.

First, add the following HTML just above the closing </body> tag:

```
<a href = "https://commons.wikimedia.
org/">Image Source: Wikimedia Commons </a>

<br>

<br>

<a href = "mybooks.html"> Check out my
favorite books! </a>
```

1. Save this file as *myanimals.html* in the *HTML Files* folder. Then view *myanimals.html* in a browser, and click on your new links to make sure they work.

2. Add one more animal image to your *myanimals.html* web page using a relative URL. Use the image *sitka-deer.jpg* from the *HTML Files* folder.

3. Next, add a link with the text "Welcome Page" and a relative URL to the file *welcome.html*.

4. Finally, add an absolute URL with the text "A fun book: *Design and Build Your Own Website*" and a link to https://lernerbooks.com/shop/show/15998.

CHAPTER 4

STYLISH FONTS AND COLORS

AS YOU'VE PROBABLY NOTICED, WEB PAGES OFTEN USE STYLISH **FONTS**, COLORFUL TEXT, AND BACKGROUND COLORS. Coders use CSS, or Cascading Style Sheets, to make the pages look engaging. A CSS file is a plain text file that holds all the information about a web page's fonts, sizes, colors, spacing, and more. It needs the extension .css. CSS files can make multiple pages of your website look similar and consistent.

You can use CSS to style your website in three main ways: inline styling, internal styling, and external style sheets. You can use inline styling for styling a single HTML element, such as a paragraph.

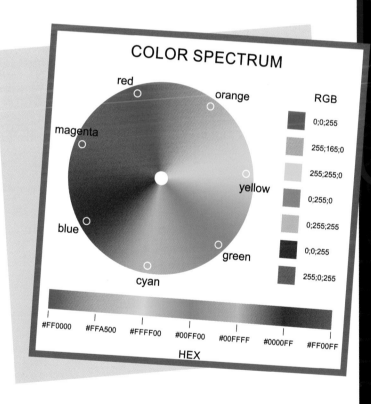

COLOR SPECTRUM

Pieces of code can also represent colors in HTML. They use a hashtag symbol, numbers, and letters. For example, #00FFF will tell your browser to display the color aqua.

If you already have a paragraph marked with
<p> in your HTML, you can style it by inserting the
keyword *style* in the opening tag of that element.
Then the paragraph tag becomes a *selector*. The
selector is any tag on the page that is selected
for styling.

```
<p style = "color: red; font-
family: Helvetica;"> This
paragraph has red text in
Helvetica font. </p>
```

If you want to style a single HTML web page, you
will use internal styles. Add the <style> and </style>
tags inside <head> and </head>.

```
<head>
<style> p { color: red; font-
family: Helvetica; } </style>
</head>
```

If you want to add the same styles to many HTML
pages, you'll use an external style sheet. The singleton
<link> tag inside <head> and </head> specifies which
external style sheet file should be used.

In this example, we have a file called *style.css* in
the same folder as the HTML file, so we are using a
relative URL.

```
<link href = "style.css" rel =
"stylesheet" type = "text/css">
```

Notice the href, rel, and type attributes in the <link> tag. The attribute href = "style.css" points to the actual file that has the style definitions. The rel stands for "relationship." It tells how the item being linked by the <link> tag is related to the current document. And the attribute type = "text/css" tells what type of link, or file, is being used.

Website coders use HTML to define the colors and other visual aspects of text and backgrounds.

CODE IT!

From your *HTML Files* folder, double-click the file *books-styled.html* to view it in your browser. Notice that the content is the same as *books.html*, with your styles and colors added.

1. Open the *style.css* file from the *HTML Files* folder. Notice the **syntax** with the curly braces and colon defining the property name and value for each selector. Pay attention to punctuation here. The colon and semicolon are important.

   ```
   selector { property-name :
   property-value;}
   ```

   ```
   Example: body { background-color:
   lightblue;}
   ```

2. Edit the *style.css* file as follows:

   Change the definition for the color of h1 from green to orange.

   Change the definition for font size for em to 18px instead of 9px.

   Change the background color of the entire web page from "lightblue" to "thistle."

3. Save the *style.css* file. View *books-styled.html* in a web browser. Did your new definitions change the appearance of this web page? Hooray! You've done it in style!

Bonus points: Use the <link> tag to link the same *style.css* style sheet to your *mybooks.html* file.

GLOSSARY

attribute: gives additional information about an element of HTML. An attribute is always specified in the opening tag.

browser: a software program for displaying HTML files from the World Wide Web

fonts: specific styles and sizes for printing or displaying letters, numbers, punctuation, and other characters

resources: text files, digital photos, audio files, or video files that can be displayed on a web page

search engines: programs that search and store web pages based on keywords to make it easy to find websites on the World Wide Web

syntax: the set of symbols and words used in a programming language

URL: the address of a file on the internet or the World Wide Web. URL stands for uniform (or universal) resource locator.

FURTHER INFORMATION

Harris, Patricia. *What Is HTML Code?* New York: PowerKids, 2018.

HTML5 Tutorial
https://www.w3schools.com/html/default.asp

Introduction to HTML
https://www.codecademy.com/learn/learn-html

Preuitt, Sheela. *Mission JavaScript.* Minneapolis: Lerner Publications, 2019.

Wainewright, Max. *I'm an HTML Web Page Builder {Build 12 Programs} HTML 5.* New York: Crabtree, 2018.

INDEX

PHOTO ACKNOWLEDGMENTS

Various screenshots by Sheela Preuitt. Additional images:
Rawpixel.com/Shutterstock.com, p. 5; Monkey Business
Images/Shutterstock.com, p. 8; screengrab from Hennepin
County Library, p. 13; Syda Productions/Shutterstock.com, p. 14;
Lerner Publishing website, www.lernerbooks.com, p. 15; Mr.
Meijer/Shutterstock.com, p. 20; daz2d/Getty Images, p. 25. Cover
and interior design elements: Bro Studio/Shutterstock.com,
(circular pattern); Leremy/Shutterstock.com (figures); Vankad/
Shutterstock.com (circuits); HuHu/Shutterstock.com (runner).